sugababes

one touch

piano • vocal • guitar

IMP

MUSIC

Folio © International Music Publications Limited
Griffin House 161 Hammersmith Road London W6 8BS England

Published 2001

Editor: Anna Joyce
Music Arranging: Artemis Music Limited Bucks SL0 0NH

www.sugababes.com

one foot in

Words and Music by Siobhan Donaghy, Mutya Buena,
Keisha Buchanan, Paul Watson, Sonia Cupid and Luke Smith

No need to call me friend I un-der-stand what you meant back then.
Not just a fling, you see I'm not your fash-ion ac-ces-so-ry.

All your time seemed to sus-pend be-tween half past se-ven and quar-ter past ten.
Time you started to think of me as more than just your girl ba-by.

overload

Words and Music by Siobhan Donaghy, Mutya Buena, Keisha Buchanan, Cameron McVey, Jony Rockstar, Felix Howard and Paul Simm

I just had to get out of there. I'm on ov - er - load
says that fate's gon - na side with me. It's been so long

in my head.
on my shelf.

Train comes, I don't know it's des - ti - na - tion. It's a

one way tick - et to a mad - man si - tu - a - tion.

Train comes, I don't know it's des - ti - na - tion.

It's a

G   F♯   *Fine*

one way tick-et to a mad - man si - tu - a - tion.

F♯

Guitar (tremolo picking)

G   F♯   **1.**   *Repeat ad lib.*

same old story

Words and Music by Siobhan Donaghy, Mutya Buena, Keisha Buchanan, Matt Rowe and John Themis

A ha,—

yeah yeah.

You had a love for me,— you said that you'd give me ev-'ry-thing.—

just let it go

**Words and Music by Siobhan Donaghy, Mutya Buena,
Keisha Buchanan, Matt Rowe and John Themis**

He was the one for me,— he made me feel al - right.

Now ev - 'ry-thing's gone wrong, we were so tight.——

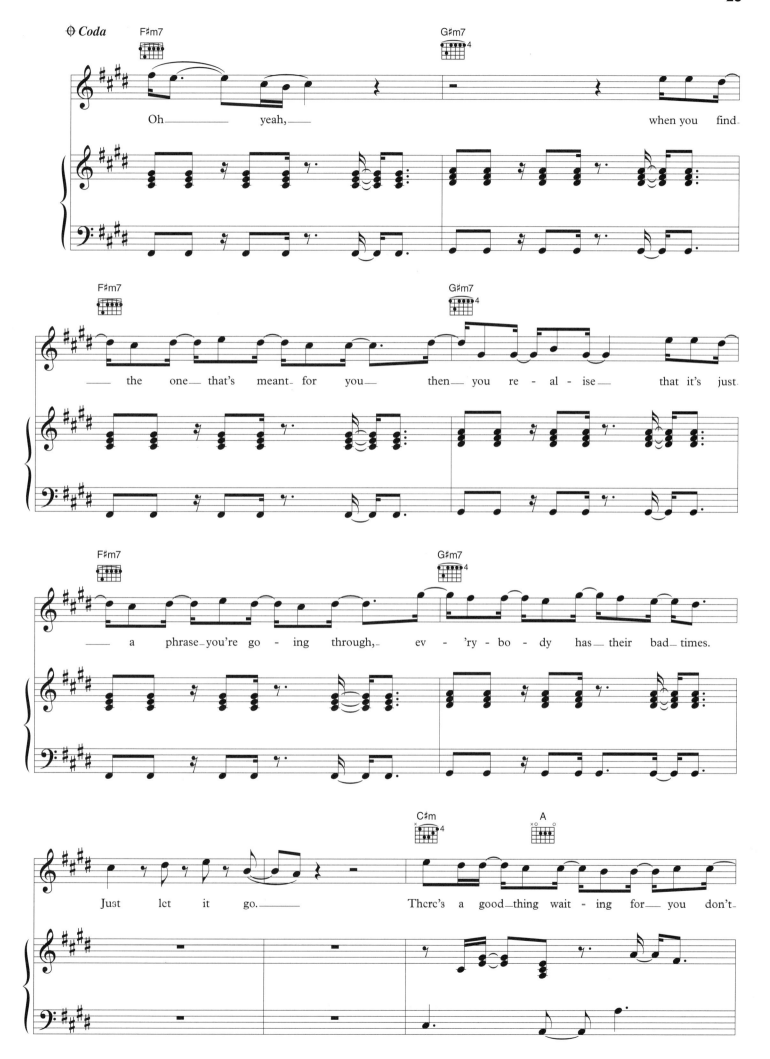

Words and Music by Siobhan Donaghy, Mutya Buena,
Keisha Buchanan, Cameron McVey, Jony Rockstar, Felix Howard and Paul Simm

(1.) know_____ I'm_____ still young, with_____ no life ex-pe-
(2.) know you are_____ my friend, but you've got to un - der - stand

- ri-ence, but can't I learn from my mis - takes, not yours?_____ Let_____
_____ that if you smo-ther me you'll on - ly end up_____ a - lone. Let_____

soul sound

Words and Music by Charlotte Edwards and Sam Harley

one touch

Words and Music by Donald McLean and Ronald Tomlinson

lush life

Words and Music by Carl MacIntosh, Yousef MacIntosh and Ronald Tomlinson

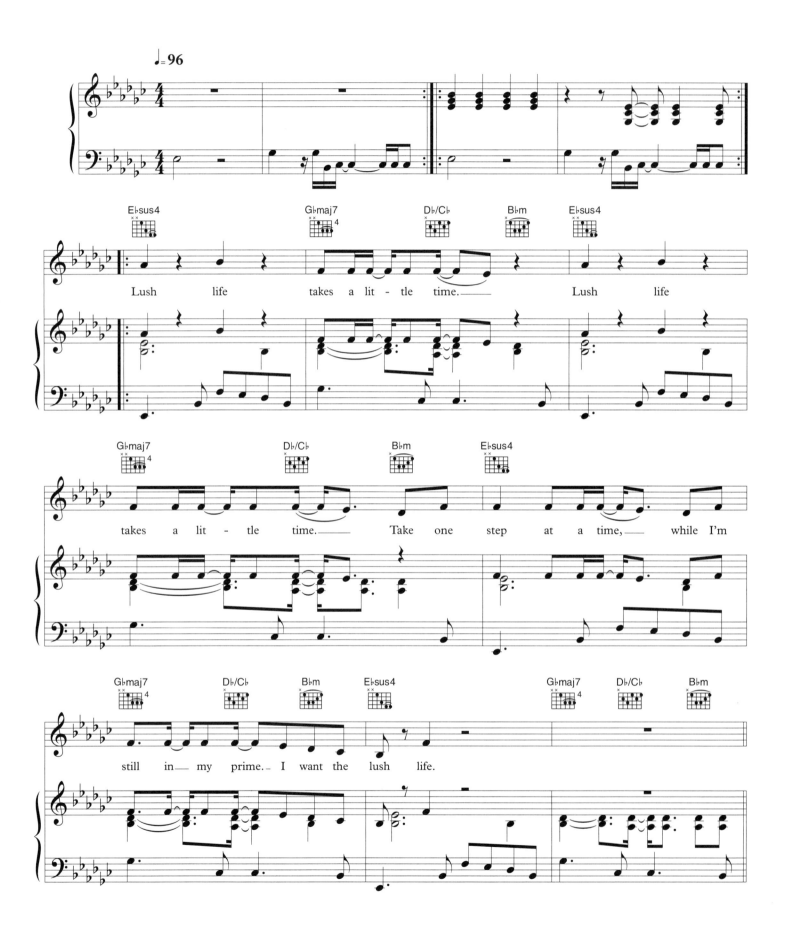

real thing

Words and Music by Siobhan Donaghy, Mutya Buena,
Keisha Buchanan, Matt Rowe and John Themis

Tell me ov-er, tell me ov-er a-gain.   Tell me ov-er, tell me ov-er a-gain.

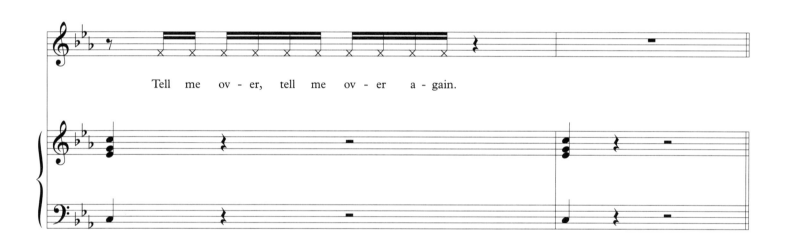

Tell me ov-er, tell me ov-er a-gain.

Hey boy,   don't you know that you're the on-ly one for   me?   Oh—— ba-by,

**Words and Music by Siobhan Donaghy, Mutya Buena, Keisha Buchanan,
Cameron McVey, Jony Rockstar, Matt Rowe and Felix Howard**

promises

Words and Music by Siobhan Donaghy, Mutya Buena, Keisha Buchanan, Cameron McVey, Jony Rockstar and Felix Howard

It's O. K. to go and make mis-takes.

It's O. K. to break your pro-mi-ses, I'm mov-in' on a-ny-way. I

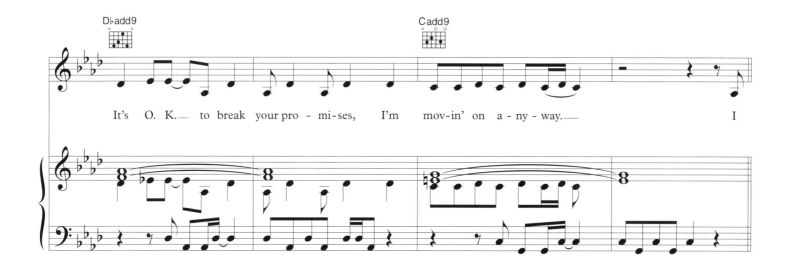

run for cover

Words and Music by Siobhan Donaghy, Mutya Buena, Keisha Buchanan, Cameron McVey, Jony Rockstar and Paul Simm